Bruno Johannsson
Christian Manifest

Aquinas Edition
2.1

The author

is a graduate economist with studies in philosophy and theology He worked in research and teaching at the University of Saarland and at private schools. He was co-author of a two volume publication about taxes and investment. Other scientific publications concerned retraining decisions and global flight. Bruno's first English publication is "Come", a volume of poetry about the Second Coming of Jesus Christ. It was translated from the German by Hilary Teske. In 2014, Bruno received the jury's award for his contribution to the Philosophy Slam, Chemnitz. He is the administrator of the website https://bruno-Johannsson.jimdofree.com.

Since 2012 he and his wife Thea are co-initiators and moderators of the Café Philo, Chemnitz. They have published five volumes of philosophical dialogues in their own neo-socratic method on the fields of social philosophy, epistemology, ethics, metaphysics and anthropology. Five of these dialogues were subjects of broadcasts of Radio Darmstadt. In "Centuries After Luther" Johannsson combines his economic, philosophical and theological expertise and outlines – contrary to postmodern mainstream and in the style of medieval Thomas von Aquin – a philosophical system on a theological basis.

Bruno Johannsson

Christian Manifest
Theses, Questions and Proposals
from "Centuries After Luther"

Translated from the German by Hilary Teske

Aquinas Edition

Bibliographic information of the German National Library: The German National Library lists this publication in the German National Bibliography; Detailed bibliographic data are available on the Internet at http://dnb.dnb.de.

Manufacturing and Publishing: BoD – Books on Demand, Norderstedt

ISBN:9 783754 346068

For Martin Luther and Joseph Smith,
to whom we possibly owe more
than we suspect.

Table of contents

II. The 95 theses in their entirety

A) Does He exist and if so, how many?
On theology

1. Eli is the supreme God of our universe.
2. Eli is immortal.
3. Eli has eternal life.
4. Eli is permeated with love and radiates love to the universe.
5. Eli lives in a specific place in the universe in the midst of a celestial civilisation created by Him.
6. Eli worked out His immortality and eternal life Himself.
7. Eli created many civilisations in our universe.
8. Eli's creations resemble primal evolution but are directed and accelerated in time.
9. Eli exercises His rule in the universe through the holders of His priesthood.
10. Eli is the first man. We are his children.
11. Jesus Christ is Eli's son in spiritual and physical respects.
12. Jesus Christ is the God of this Earth under Eli's direction
13. Jesus Christ assisted in creating Earth and plays the central role in perfecting it.
14. Jesus Christ is the same person as Jehovah (Jahweh).
15. Jesus Christ atoned for the sins of the world.
16. Faith in Jesus Christ makes eternal life possible.
17. The Holy Ghost has a spiritual body in God's image.
18. The Holy Ghost "mothers" the Saints.
19. Lucifer is one of Eli's spiritual sons, rebelled against his Father and was expelled from heaven.
20. Satan and his devils do not have bodies of flesh and bones but can enter such bodies under certain conditions.
21. Satan and his devils are indestructible spiritual beings.
22. Satan and his armies cause the evil on this Earth as long and as far as Eli allows them to.
23. There are many gods, but only Eli is allowed to be worshipped.

24. Every person on Earth has the possibility of becoming a god.

25. Human history is a drama unfolding under Eli's direction, in which the actors play themselves without knowing their roles completely.

26. The fall of Adam, the first and second coming of Christ and the Last Judgement are the central events of human history.

27. Under Eli's direction, Jehovah has steered human history by means of revelation and personal intervention.

28. In God's view, human history is marked by alternating apostasy and restoration.

29. In the final millennium Christ will preside on Earth and lead His people to perfection.

30. The unchaining and rechaining of the adversary, the Last Judgement and the transformation of Earth will take place at the end of the millennium.

B) What is truth and how can I find it?
On the theory of knowledge

1 Truth is the particularity of an image of something that represents its being as well as possible with regard to a specific objective.

2 Every language generates and restricts possibilities of creating true images.

3. An improvement in the state of knowledge in many cases requires an improvement in language.

4. A person's knowledge is greater, the more favourable the balance of true and false images is in their mind.

5. Knowledge can be acquired through communication or research.

6. All knowledge that will ever exist on Earth existed in the universe before planet Earth was created.

7. The research methods devised to date are not sufficient to generate all vital knowledge.

8. Divine revelation is the form of communication with the greatest chances and risks.

9. Eli has given every person a conditional promise of receiving personal revelation.

10. Perfect knowledge of something requires superior intelligence of the knower over the known, or at least equal intelligence.

C) The cone of knowledge
On the theory of science

1. Every phenomenon is in principle the subject of science.

2. How narrowly the term "science" is apprehended depends on the claims made on the methods and results of science.

3. The system of the sciences can be depicted as an expanding cone.

4. Philosophy forms the tip of the science cone.

5. Theology is the science with the greatest potential to influence other sciences.

D) Sprit and matter
On a theory of spirit

1. Spirit is the smallest component of matter.

2. Spirit is contained in all components of matter hitherto scientifically proven.

3. Spiritual elements have the character of chips.

4. There are at least two types of spiritual elements.

5. Spiritual elements can be organised into spiritual bodies.

6. Spiritual bodies can be free or bound within physical bodies.

7. Free spiritual bodies can move in solid, liquid or gaseous substances.

E. Accelerated and directed evolution
On cosmology

1. The fundamental principle of our universe is the love of God.
2. There is a large number of different civilisations in the universe.
3. In the universe there is or was a primal earth, on which life developed through full evolution.
4. Our Earth is a – possibly modified – copy of planets already existing in the universe.
5. Prior to the formation of the Earth's natural structures, the related spiritual structures already existed.
6. Our Earth is a mix of divine intervention and natural evolution.
7. Our Earth is destined to become a celestial system.

F. Highly developed ape or Eli's child?
On anthropology

1. Every mortal human after Adam is a dual being.
2. A mortal human is a caricature of their eternal identity.
3. A human is a microcosmic image of society.
4. Subjectively perceived freedom is based on a lack of self-knowledge.
5. Human life is a drama in which the main actors do not know their roles.

G) A state in miniature
On psychology and medicine

1. There are at least two parties in every soul.

2. The ego is the central organ of the soul.
3. Perfection requires willingness to forgo health and life.
4. Holistic and sustainable help must take account of the interdependence of an individual's emanations and strengthen their ego.

H) What should we do?
On ethics

1. Good is what corresponds to God's will in a certain situation.
2. Any deed that fulfils the conditions of all-embracing love is good.
3. God's commandments bridge the deficits of the respective state of science.
4. God's commandments are like stars in the night on the way to the highest summit.
5. Love is the mother of all other virtues.
6. Family bonds can be heavenly bonds.
7. Anyone who simply lets themselves go can easily fall into a trap.
8. The royal way is a narrow path through valleys of humility to summits of joy.
9. Freedom is not unbounded even above the clouds.
10. To everyone their own world!
I. Space, time and everything in it.
On totology

1. The Garden of Eden can serve as a model of a closed, static and harmonious civilisation.
2. The degree of harmony in a civilisation depends on the ideologies of those active in it to a great extent.
3. Pluralism and multiculturalism are cornerstones of lived spiritual freedom.

4. Government authorities should behave as neutrally as possible in the competition of ideologies.

J. What attracts us?
On aesthetics and cultural philosophy

1. The multiplicity of cultures is based on a broad spectrum of aesthetic inclinations, which are partly stamped by ideology.
2. The classic ideal of good, truth and beauty will mark the culture of the millennium.

K. The global royal way
On economics and political science

1. More goods can sometimes mean less welfare.
2. The emotionally suggestive parts of product advertising are ethically questionable.
3. A positive work-leisure balance can lead to a considerable enhancement of welfare.
4. Dramatic gains in welfare can be achieved on all levels by redistribution.
5. Global elimination of death from poverty needs to have much higher priority.
6. Rights of self-determination need to be further developed on all levels in all nations.
7. Fair rules for international competition of ideologies should be established worldwide and enforced by the UNO.
8. Democracy and free-market economy are important transitional forms on the way to the millennium.
9. Democrats of all countries unite!
10. Economic progress should not have losers in the long run.
11. The Marxist principle 'From each according to his ability, to each according to his need' can only be realized in a civilization characterized by love.

III. The theses with their questions and proposals

A) Does He exist and if so, how many?
On theology

Thesis 1. Eli is the supreme God of our universe.

Open questions:
1. How far does Eli's power extend in our universe? For instance, does He also have power to influence the expansion of the universe?
2. Do parallel universes exist and if so, are they also subject to Eli's authority?
3. Does the hierarchy of the gods have more than two levels and if so, how do the levels differ?

Thesis 2. Eli is immortal

Open questions:
1. Can an immortal being deliberately bring about a temporary separation of body and spirit? For example, after His resurrection can Jesus Christ still appear as a spirit, thus temporarily divesting Himself of His body?
2. In which way are the spirit body and the physical body interlocked?
3. Can an immortal, resurrected being walk through walls, as we normally presume a pure spirit is able to?
4. Is there any kind of metabolism in an immortal body? What part is played by the blood vessels and organs of excretion?
5. What properties of chemical and physical information does the light that pervades and envelops Eli have?
6. To what extent can information and attitudes be communicated by the light emanating from Eli's presence?

Thesis 3. Eli has eternal life

Open questions:
   1. What technologies does Eli employ to move around the universe?
   2. Is it true that Eli can only be in one place at one time?
   3. What possibilities does Eli have to adapt His body to non-heavenly conditions?
   4. What properties does Eli's sexuality have and what part does it play in His life?
   5. What dimensions does eternal increase have and what part does Eli play in it?

Thesis 4. Eli is permeated with love and radiates love to the universe.

Open questions
   1. In what way is love sealed in Eli so that He also remains in it or must remain in it?
   2. What is the mixture of rationality and emotionality in His divine love?
   3. Is Eli equal to the other Gods in love or is His love greater or the greatest?

Thesis 5. Eli lives in a specific place in the universe in the midst of a celestial civilisation created by Him.

Open questions
   1. In which galaxy is the celestial body where Eli reigns over the universe?
   2. What are the natural scientific features of this body?
   3. To what degree is the heavenly civilisation hierarchical?
   4. Does the absence of privacy apply only from top to bottom but also from bottom to top?

5. What are the roles of sexuality, marriage and family in this civilisation?

6. Is the heavenly civilisation a "stationary system"[1]?

Thesis 6. Eli worked out His immortality and eternal life Himself.

Thesis 7. Eli created many civilisations in our universe.

Open questions

1. How far-reaching is the scope of Jesus's atonement in Jerusalem? Does it only relate to all the people who will have lived on Earth or does it include beings in the other creations?

2. What position does our Earth have among all Eli's creations? Is it one of the many countless or does it play a more central role?

Thesis 8. Eli's creations resemble primal evolution but are directed and accelerated in time.

Open questions

1. What was before the creation of the universe?

2. How did intelligence come into play, of which it has been revealed that it cannot be created?

3. Is love as an attribute inseparably connected with intelligence?

4. Is evil itself also a form of intelligence, or its antithesis?

---

[1] This is a model concept discussed in economics of a world without growth or shrinkage. The processes occurring in it are circular. Eli says to this effect: My path is an eternal round. This indicates the stationary nature of His central civilisation. The concept of eternal increase, as taught in Latter-day Saint doctrine, could refer to this universe.

Thesis 9. Eli exercises His rule in the universe through the holders of His priesthood.

Thesis 10. Eli is the first man. We are His children.

Open questions:
1. How did the first man become the first God?
2. Do all or only a limited number of God's childen have the hereditary disposition to become gods?

Thesis 11. Jesus Christ is Eli's son in spiritual and physical respects.

Open questions

1. In what way are children spiritually conceived and born?

2. What part does Jesus Christ play in the creation of the worlds made before Earth?

3. Is it appropriate to describe Maria's conception as "immaculate"?

Thesis 12. Jesus Christ is the God of this Earth under Eli's direction.

Thesis 13. Jesus Christ assisted in creating Earth and plays the central role in perfecting it.

Thesis 14. Jesus Christ is the same person as Jehovah (Jahweh).

Open questions

1. Was it Jesus Christ who fought with Jacob?
2. Was it Jesus Christ who gave the Ten Commandments?
3. Were the prophecies about the Messiah inspired by the Father and/or the Holy Ghost?

Thesis 15. Jesus Christ atoned for the sins of all people.

Open questions

1. Did the original plan for this Earth have to be altered after Lucifer had rebelled and been expelled from heaven with his hosts?
2. Is the atonement of Jesus Christ only effective for people on Earth or also for creatures in all other worlds?

Thesis 16. Faith in Jesus Christ makes eternal life possible

Thesis 17. The Holy Ghost has a spiritual body in God's image.

Open questions

1. What role did the Holy Ghost play in the pre-earth world (= pre-existence)?[2]
2. Is the Holy Ghost on the same level as Jesus Christ in the hierarchy beneath the Father?
3. Is the sex of the Holy Ghost male or female?
4. Will the Holy Ghost be on Earth in the millennium and be married and have a family?

---

[2] All souls who will ever have lived here on earth are literally spiritually conceived sons and daughters of God and already existed as such in the pre-earthly spirit world.

Thesis 18. The Holy Ghost "mothers" the Saints.

Open questions

1. Does every person have at least one guardian angel or is this a particular privilege of members of the Church of Jesus Christ?

2. Can the Holy Ghost prompt a person to make exceptions or compromises in applying God's laws?

3. What is the division of labour between Father, Son and Holy Ghost in performing miracles: are they all or only some performed by the power of the Holy Ghost?

4. Does the power of the Holy Ghost also play a part in destruction?

Thesis 19. Lucifer is one of Eli's spiritual sons, rebelled against his Father and was expelled from heaven.

Open questions

1. Did Jesus Christ's plan of salvation imply the existence of evil as an alternative choice and, if so, who was supposed to represent evil, since Lucifer had not fallen at that time?

2. Did Jesus Christ's plan include the Garden of Eden and the fall of Adam and Eve as one of its phases?

3. With what means is war waged in the spirit world?

4. Will Satan and his devils be given another chance to reconcile themselves with Eli?

Thesis 20. Satan and his devils do not have bodies of flesh and bones but can enter such bodies under certain conditions.

Open questions

1. Under what conditions does God permit evil spirits to enter a person or dwell permanently in them?

2. Has this already happened in children under 8 years of age and if so, for what reason?

3. Can evil spirits be permanently cast out of a person exclusively with medication?

Thesis 21. Satan and his minions are indestructible spiritual beings.

Thesis 22. Satan and his armies cause the evil on Earth as long and as far as Eli allows them to.

Open questions:

1. Are all the spirits that decided against God in the pre-earth world working on Earth?

2. Can intelligence be ascribed to evil spirits or only such attributes as strength of purpose, sophistication, hatred, cruelty, etc.?

3. What are the restrictions Eli has imposed on the work of the evil spirits?

Thesis 23. There are many gods, but only Eli is allowed to be worshipped.

Open questions

1. What is exactly the common characteristic of all beings in the hierarchy of the Gods?

2. What role do women play in the hierarchy of the Gods?

Do they have the status of female deities? In which respect are they equal and in which not equal to the Gods?

Thesis 24. Every person on Earth has the possibility of becoming a god.

Open questions
1. Have the evil spirits all been irrevocably disinherited in the above sense?
2. When did Jesus Christ receive the state of deity as His inheritance – already in the pre-earth world, at His birth, after His atoning sacrifice or not until after His resurrection?
3. To what extent is existence in the terrestrial and telestial worlds also marked by the spirit of love?

Thesis 25. Human history is a drama unfolding under Eli's direction, in which the actors play themselves without knowing their roles completely.

Open Question
1. Is there a custom in Judaism and Islam that a father gives his children a fatherly blessing, at the latest on his deathbed?

Thesis 26. The fall of Adam, the first and second coming of Christ and the Last Judgement are the central events of human history.

Thesis 27. Under Eli's direction, Jehovah has steered human history by means of revelation and personal intervention.

Open questions
1. To what extent is it historically reasonable to view the two World Wars in the 20th century as a single entity? What historical insights can we gain by doing this?

2. What lasting global changes in ideological, cultural, social (including demographic), political and economic respects took place between 1914 and 1950?

3. How much time would these changes probably have taken or would they have taken place at all if the cataclysms of war had not occurred? (It is clear to me that this question is very hypothetical and a scientific analysis is scarcely possible.)

Thesis 28. In God's view, human history is marked by alternating apostasy and restoration.

Open questions:

1. When and how did the apostasy prophesied by Paul take place?

2. How and to what extent was the apostles' priesthood authority preserved after their deaths?

3. Was the Church already decadent in its roots when it was elevated to the state religion in the Roman Empire?

4. Did the Roman Catholic Church receive apostolic authority and if so, was it able to maintain it despite complex political relations, corruption, inquisition and such practices as the indulgence regulation, which Luther rightly denounced?[3]

5. How are we to judge the diverse secessions from the Catholic Church with regard to the preservation of authority and doctrine?

------

[3] In principle, I consider this possible, since ancient Israel also apostasised and was untrue from time to time, without thereby losing priesthood authority. The poor state of His Church is still no compelling reason for the Lord to withdraw His authority. However, He may not have wanted to leave it on Earth at all after the death of the last apostle; otherwise He would have arranged for the quorum of the twelve apostles to be preserved.

6. Was God able to regard the agglomeration of Christian currents existing at the beginning of the 19th century as "His Church" or was one of the many churches "His Church"?

Thesis 29. In the final millennium Christ will preside on Earth and lead His people to perfection.

Open questions:

1. What will be the dimensions of the Old Jerusalem in the millennium?

2. How many and what nations will live outside the two Jerusalems in the millennium?

3. What will be the intellectual state of these civilisations? What ideologies will they cultivate?

4. What cultural, scientific and political relations will exist between the Holy Cities and the must larger remainder of Earth?

5. In what way will Jesus Christ exert influence on the nations outside the two Jerusalems?

6. Will all inhabitants of the holy civilisations be immortal?

7. Will immortal souls still go through a learning process towards eternal life in the millennium?

8. Will there still be increase within or outside the holy cities?

9. Will there be markets in the New and Old Jerusalem and if so, how will they function so as not to violate the law of love?

Thesis 30. The unchaining and rechaining of the adversary, the Last Judgement and the transformation of Earth are the last events of the history of this mankind.

Open questions

1. How wll the nations outside Zion develop during the millennium?

2. Will the final great war be waged only with spiritual or also with physical weapons?

3. Will Satan still appear as plaintiff at the Last Judgement?

B) What is truth and how do I find it?
On the theory of knowledge

Thesis 1. Truth is the particularity of an image of something that represents its being as well as possible with regard to a specific objective.

Thesis 2. Every language generates and restricts possibilities of creating true images.

Open questions

1. What connection exists between individual linguistic dyanamics and intelligence?

2. What linguistic features promote or impede acquisition of knowledge?

3. According to latter-day revelation, Adam had a particularly "pure language." What were its characteristics?

Thesis 3. An improvement in the state of knowledge in many cases requires an improvement in language.

Thesis 4. A person's knowledge is greater, the more favourable the balance of true and false images is in their mind.

Thesis 5. Knowledge can be acquired through communication or research.

Thesis 6. All knowledge that will ever exist on Earth existed in the universe before planet Earth was created.

Open questions

1. A considerable part of knowledge is of only temporary importance in human history. Was this temporarily relevant knowledge also already stored before Earth was created?

2. What role did good spirits play in the invention of the atomic bomb?

7. The research methods devised to date are not sufficient to generate all vital knowledge.

8. Divine revelation is the form of communication with the greatest chances and risks.

9. Eli has given every person a conditional promise of receiving personal revelation.

10. Perfect knowledge of something requires superior intelligence of the knower over the known, or at least equal intelligence.

C) The cone of knowledge
On the theory of knowledge

Thesis 1. Every phenomenon is in principle the subject of science.

Thesis 2. How narrowly the term "science" is apprehended depends on the claims made on the methods and results of science.

Thesis 3. The system of the sciences can be depicted as an expanding cone.

Thesis 4. Philosophy forms the tip of the science cone.

Proposal

It would be desirable for research institutes, scientific journals and renowned scientists of all disciplines to state their approach on their websites by disclosing their philosophical profile, which includes the unquestioned fundaments of their research. This would promote the consistency of the cone of science from its base to its tip.

Thesis 5. Theology is the science with the greatest potential to influence other sciences.

Open question

How great is the relative influence of the world religions on the global scientific development over the centuries?

D) Spirit and matter
On a theory of spirit[4]

Thesis 1. Spirit is the smallest component of matter.

Open questions

1. Are there various kinds of spirit elements with different functions, different sizes, structures, etc.?

2. Can spirit elements appear as particles and/or waves?

3. What is the relation between spirit elements and light?

4. Can the aura phenomenon be scientifically proved and how does it come about?

Thesis 2. Spirit is contained in all components of matter hitherto scientifically proven.

Open questions

1. Provided there is actually at least one spirit element contained in the particles of coarse matter, how is it anchored?

2. In which way is it connected information-wise with the particles of coarse matter in which it is located?

3. In which way is it connected information-wise with the spirit elements of the other particles of coarse matter?

---

[4] I deliberately do not speak of a theory of mind. In the cone of knowledge my theory of spirit should be placed in the border area of the natural sciences and humanities. I also would not deny some relationships to esoteric and spiritology.

Thesis 3. Spirit elements have the character of microchips.

Open questions
1. Are scientific instruments of observation conceivable to make spirit elements visible or is this ruled out per se? [5]
2. Are there analogies between the multiplicity of body cells and the multiplicity of spirit elements?
3. According to Joseph Smith (see above), a pure spirit body is also able to perceive other spirit bodies with its "senses." Is it also able to identify spirit elements?

Thesis 4. There are at least two kinds of spirit elements

Open questions
1. Are there connections between positive and negative electric charges and bright and dark spirit elements?
2. What role do the kinds of spirit elements play in the unfolding of light in the spectrum of colours?
3. What happened to the dark cloud surrounding Joseph Smith: was it dispelled, dissolved or transformed?
4. Is there a connection between the dark spirit elements and the so-called dark matter which makes up the greater part of the matter in the universe?
5. Is there a connection between dark spirit elements and the black holes in the universe?

Thesis 5. Spirit elements can be organised into spirit bodies.

---

[5] For instance, because it is possible that coarse matter can never reproduce fine spirit matter, as Joseph Smith suggests in the quotation above.

Open questions

1. How was our spirit body, i.e. our soul created?

2. Was there a development of our soul in the pre-earth world and if so, how was it effected and what kind of changes did it generate?

3. In what way are the elements of our spirit body connected with one another?

4. Does our spirit body have a specific number of elements, just as our physical body has a specific number of cells?

Thesis 6. Spirit bodies can be free or bound within physical bodies.

Thesis 7. Free spirit bodies can move in solid, liquid and gaseous substances.

E) Accelerated and directed evolution
On cosmology

Thesis 1. The fundamental principle of our universe is the love of God.

Open questions

1. Are all souls in the celestial worlds perfect in love or are there different degrees of love?

2. What role does love play in the terrestrial and telestial worlds?

3. Is there a small spark of love in the soul of Satan or a devil?

4. Are the realms of darkness sealed off from God's love or is it able to penetrate them?

Thesis 2. There is a large number of different civilisations in the universe.

Open questions

1. How many births have there been globally since the year 0 of the Jewish calendar?

2. Is there a connection between the "outer darkness" of holy scripture and dark matter or black holes?

3. What is the difference in the structures of dark and "bright matter" which we can observe through our telescopes?

Thesis 3. In the universe there is or was a primal earth, on which life was created through full evolution.

Open questions

1. How did the universe come into existence and what was before its genesis?

2. How did life in our universe originate?

3. Why does our Earth also have evolutionary traces if it was actually modelled on a planet that had already completed its evolution? Why imitate the various stages of development in the new creation?

Thesis 4. Our Earth is a copy of planets already existing in the universe.

Thesis 5. Prior to the formation of the Earth's natural structures, the related spirit structures already existed.

Thesis 6. Our Earth is a mix of divine intervention and natural evolution.

Open questions
   1. Which laws did God find in the universe and which did He Himself alter or establish?
   2. How does the biblical account of Creation go along with modern research regarding timing and content? Where are there incongruities or compatibilities?
   3. How do natural cosmic or terrestrial disasters and climate changes alter the conditions for determining the ages of fossils and other findings? Might there be burning or freezing processes with extreme temperatures which distort assessment of age or even make it impossible?

Thesis 7. Our Earth is destined to become a celestial system.

Open questions
1. Will

1. Will Earth remain in its current solar system after its exaltation and what will happen to this system when Earth is transformed?[6]

2. Which physical, chemical and biological properties will the celestial space sector of Earth have as a whole?

3. Will the celestial space sector of Earth be immortal in the sense that it will not decay as so many systems in the universe do?

---

[6] It is interesting that in his Divine Comedy Dante links his ten levels of the heavenly world, which he rather vaguely calls "paradiso" in contrast to "inferno" and "purgatorio," to the planets in the solar system. This probably originated more from his fantasy than from a revelation. As far as I know, he does not claim to have been divinely inspired in his otherwise important literary work. (Cf. Dante Alighieri, The Divine Comedy, 1320, translation by Henry Wadsworth Longfellow, 1867,
http://en.wikisource.org/wiki/The_Divine_Comedy

F. Highly developed ape or Eli's child?
On anthropology

Thesis 1. Every mortal human after Adam is a dual being.

Open questions

1. How far do the above statements also apply to beings similar to humans that are not descended from Adam?

2. How far do the above statements apply to animals?

3. How does the body-soul relationship change in the course of a life? What does "adulthood" mean in this context?

4. How do addictions, sickness, etc. affect the body-soul relationship?

5. What impact do alcohol, soft and hard drugs and psychotropic drugs have on the body-soul relationship?

Thesis 2. A mortal human is a caricature of their eternal identity.

Thesis 3. A human being is a microcosmic image of a national economy.

Open questions

1. Does an ego or self exist and if so, how is it bound to the nervous system?

2. How do the interdependent influences of soul and body take place and what role does the ego play in this?

Thesis 4. Subjectively perceived freedom is based on a lack of self-knowledge.

Thesis 5. Every human life is a drama where the main actor does not know their role.

G. A state in miniature
On psychology and medicine

Thesis 1. There are at least two "parties" in every soul.[7]

Thesis 2. The ego is the central organ of the soul.

Open questions

1. It would be interesting to know if the phenomenon exists with the mentally ill that several voices can speak from

---

[7] Common parlance sees individuals rather than groups here. Thus, some people analyse their own behaviour by ascribing it to the influence of their "inner couch potato". (Cf. Thea and Bruno Johannsson: What is a human being? Philosophische Dialoge [Philosophical Dialogues]. 2nd dialogue. Unpublished manuscript.) Of course, the inner couch potato also needs an antagonist, which is, however, seldom named. My wife suggests "inner overachiever" as a designation for this. Another pair of expressions might be "epicure" and "striver." An example might be: "My striver won't let me rest. I have to prepare for my public appearance tomorrow", etc. At this point I would like to refer to the words Goethe places in Faust's mouth: "Zwei Seelen wohnen, ach! in meiner Brust, die eine will sich von der andern trennen; die eine hält, in derber Liebeslust, sich an die Welt mit klammernden Organen; die andre hebt gewaltsam sich vom Dust zu den Gefilden hoher Ahnen [Two souls alas! are dwelling in my breast; and each is fain to leave its brother. The one, fast clinging, to the world adheres with clutching organs, in love's sturdy lust; the other strongly lifts itself from dust to yonder high, ancestral spheres.]." (Cf. Johann Wolfgang von Goethe, 1831, Faust, lines 112-117. Full text in German and English side-by-side translations: Priest, Brooks and Coleridge, 2013.) Here Goethe is certainly alluding to what is important to me. However, I would not like to speak of two souls in my philosophical context. A human being also has only one soul. Consequently, it must be a question of conflicting inclinations within the one soul, in this case Faust's soul.

37

the person at the same time and if, in the case of possession by more than one spirit, all the sounds are, in principle, uttered outward through a speech organ.

2. Linguistically, it would be interesting to investigate if there are languages in which a reflexive personal relationship, for instance "it is clear to me," "I speak to myself," "I must pull myself together" cannot be expressed, and if so, which languages they are.

3. What are the common features and differences between my remarks and the concept of "it," "I" and "super-ego," represented by Sigmund Freud and his disciples?

Thesis 3. Perfection requires willingness to forgo health and life.

Thesis 4. Holistic and sustainable help must take account of the interdependence of an individual's emanations and strengthen their ego.

Proposals
1. Further development of the profession of life counsellor. In the professional training, instruction in the basics of psychosomatics and micro-economics should be provided as well as knowledge of psychology, psychotherapy and relationships therapy.

2 It should be examined if, given specific indications, the medical insurance organisations could support holistic life counselling financially.

3. It should be examined to what extent the qualification of counsellor could or should be extended in the job centres.

4. Increased integration of holistic life counselling into the educational system (primary and middle schools, grammar schools, vocational schools, universities, adult education centres, etc.)

5. Revision of the curricula of state schools concerning their holistic approach so as to possibly learn from school models such as those of the Waldorf/Steiner schools.

H. What should we do?
On ethics

Thesis 1. Good is what corresponds to God's will in a certain situation.

Thesis 2. Any deed that fulfils the conditions of all-embracing love is good.

Open questions
1. Is an action already good when it is motivated by love of others with no consideration of love of self?
2. Is the result of an action optimal for all those involved – possibly even for the community – when it is consistent with love of self, love of others and the golden rule?
3. Under what conditions is the tridimensional commandment to love a maxim compatible with Kant's categorical imperative?

Thesis 3. God's commandments bridge the deficits of the respective state of science.

Thesis 4. God's commandments are like stars in the night on the way to the highest summit.

Thesis 5. Love is the mother of all other virtues.

Thesis 6. Family bonds can be heavenly bonds.

Open questions

1. To what extent does the transition from sporadic same-sex relationships with alternating partners to a permanent commitment to a same-sex partner constitute ethical progress?

2. Does a sublimation of sexuality in Plato's sense open the door to more love in sexuality?

3. In a psycho-physical respect, what distinguishes a sexuality marked by love from a sexuality that gives a free rein to physical and mental instincts?

4. Is it possible, as a partner, to be filled with the pure love of Christ and still to experience the sexual tension that makes sexual intercourse possible?

Thesis 7. Anyone who simply lets themselves go can easily fall into a trap.

Open question

Are there meaningful relaxation possibilities, on the one hand, and dangerous ones, on the other, or is everything that is fun equally risky because it can lead to addiction or one-sidedness?[8]

Thesis 8. The royal way is a narrow path through valleys of humility to peaks of joy

---

[8] That is a question suggested to me by Thea Johannsson, which I have slightly reformulated.

Thesis 9. Freedom is not unbounded even above the clouds.

Open question
Can we speak of law and obedience when freedom to break the law no longer exists and the soul is sealed in the law?

Thesis 10. To everyone their own world!

Open questions
1. How much freedom should children and adolescents be allowed to choose their ideology in home upbringing and school education? How should the amount of freedom be adjusted to the various age brackets?
2. Are there types of parental intervention in children's mental development that should be prohibited by law?

Proposal
1. Children over the age of seven and adolescents who are not yet of an age to choose their religion should be given several opportunities to gain an overview of all world ideologies. This can be done in school projects or public ideological fairs. It might be possible to establish permanent exhibitions for all ideologies wishing to present themselves.

I. Space, time and everything in it.
On totology[9]

Thesis 1. The Garden of Eden can serve as a model of a closed, static and harmonious civilisation.

Thesis 2. The degree of harmony in a civilisation depends on the ideologies of those active in it to a great extent.

Thesis 3. Pluralism and multiculturalism are cornerstones of lived spiritual freedom.

Open questions

1. What connection should be established in a civilisation between the size of a majority or minority and its social rights and duties?

2. What questions are so critical for the identity of a civilisation that decisions about them should be the subject of a referendum? (Example: limitation of immigration to Switzerland.)

3. How much freedom should there be for the enemies of freedom?

Proposals

Harassment, persecution, imprisonment or even killing of people who abandon an ideology should be explicitly prohib-

---

[9] As I do not know of any comparable approach, I propose this term for an analytical method in which the subject is the entire contents of a space-time sector (Latin totum). If at least one human being is living in this sector, I speak of a civilisation. What this means exactly will be explained in the next four theses. However, the subsequent theses will also make indirect use of this approach. Any extremely comprehensive historical analysis constitutes an approximation to this concept.

ited in the UN Charter and the measure enforced worldwide with UNO means.

Thesis 4. Government authorities should behave as neutrally as possible in the competition of ideologies.

Open questions

1. In what way should the human rights to freedom of opinion and religion be specified so that the true spectrum of membership in ideologies can be tendentially established worldwide?

2. According to scientific estimates, how high would the income from the contributions by members of the Protestant and Catholic churches in Germany be (approx. €10bn. in 2012) if the members paid their contributions on their own initiative without automatic withholding of the tax and or government coercion?

3. What knowledge and concepts of economic theory of competition might be used for competition of ideologies?

Proposals

1. More intensive, more objective and fairer communication between ideologies would be desirable on local, regional, national and global levels ("ideological mix") to establish intersections of and differences in convictions in a way comprehensible to all.

2. Get rid of government collection of church tax and do not replace it! Instead, possibly equal subsidising of social initiatives, such as the – still inadequate – subsidies to private schools.

J) What draws us onwords?
On aesthetics and cultural philosophy

Thesis 1. The multiplicity of cultures is based on a broad spectrum of aesthetic inclinations, which are partly stamped by ideology.

Open questions

1. Is their scientific evidence of principles concerning the connection between people's theoretical, ethical and aesthetic judgements?

2. Overall, has there been a strengthening or weakening of the global cultural identity during the last few decades?

Thesis 2. The classic ideal of good, truth and beauty will mark the culture of the millennium.

K) The global royal way.
On economics and political science

Thesis 1. More goods may sometimes mean less welfare.

Thesis 2. The emotionally suggestive parts of product advertising are ethically questionable.

Open questions

1. What statistical connection exists between individual income or wealth, on the one hand, and the incidence of addictions, on the other?

2. What does the economic benefit-cost analysis of emotionally suggestive advertising look like?

Proposals

1. Ban on commercial advertising in public space, i.e. in the street, in town squares, on roads, etc.

2. Ban on commercials during individual television programs and directly before and after children's programs.

Thesis 3. A positive work-leisure balance can lead to a considerable gain in welfare.

Questions

1. How many people worldwide have to bear a continual unreasonably negative impact of their work on their leisure and how does this impact come about?

2. How many people feel extremely good at their workplaces and for what reasons?

3. From the viewpoint of working people on all levels (including bosses and managers), what working conditions need

to exist for realising an optimal combination of productivity and wellbeing?

Proposals

1. It should be prescribed in labour law that active bullying and bossy behaviour at work, at whatever level in the organisation, are grounds for dismissal or complaint.

2. It should be considered if bossy behaviour, bullying and tolerance of such behaviours on the part of superiors should not be made criminal offences and punished accordingly, e.g. with fines amounting to one or several months' salary depending on the severity of the case. To avoid overloading the labour courts, arbitration tribunals could be established in large companies as part of employee participation.

Thesis 4. The welfare of nations can be increased dramatically just by redistribution processes.

Open questions:

1. What parts of Adam Smith's theory have proved themselves empirically in the last two centuries and which were rather refuted or questioned?

2. To what extent did Adam Smith stimulate economic research by laying foundations for the development of theories which had and still have predictive power?

3. How high is the value of still usable food which is thrown away annually worldwide? How many people could be saved from starvation for a year with this money?

4. What role does corruption play in the 30 poorest countries of the world?

5. Assuming we would like to raise a certain income through a uniform global tax in order to eradicate death from starvation within ten years, what advantages and disad-

vantages would the amusement tax I propose have compared with a wealth tax?[10]

Proposals

1. All governments of the world reduce their annual defense budgets by 1% and transfer the money saved to the UN organisation "Swords to Ploughshares" (yet to be founded) with the purpose of promoting agricultural production in the areas where people are starving.

2. All nations of the earth impose a uniform amusement tax of maximally 1% of the quoted consumption share to be paid by the supplying companies. The receipts serve the sole purpose of eradicating death from starvation on Earth.

Thesis 5. Global elimination of death from poverty needs to have much higher priority.

Proposals

1. Every country with an incidence of death due to poverty should be assigned a rich country as a development partner. The latter coordinates all global activities for the benefit of the structurally weak country and provides it with a scientific foundation. The goal is a long-term partnership of equals in politics, economy and culture.

2. Non-commercial organisations, including public administration and charitable organisations, should be subject to external quality control with certification, as are numerous

---

[10] This question would require a careful economic analysis which I am not able to undertake here. The amusement tax is imposed on a certain group of consumer spending. The wealth tax is imposed on retained assets and indirectly penalizes savings and investments. There is extensive discussion by experts concerning this topic.

companies. This also applies to EU and UN organisations, particularly those which are in charge of development aid.

Thesis 6. Rights of self-determination need to be further developed on all levels in all nations.

Open questions

1. How does a holistic[11] comparison of the development of Norway and Switzerland, on the one hand, and comparable members of the EU, on the other, turn out, also considering the financial market and debt crises?

2. What impact on welfare did the dissolution of the Soviet Union have on the populations of the resulting states, including Russia?

3 Does the current political structure of the world allow a statement to be made on the connection between the size of a macro-civilisation and its (holistic) welfare?

4. Are historic statements to be found concerning the connection over the centuries between the size of a macro-civilisation and its welfare? (Extreme example: Roman Empire versus Greek city states.)

5. What does the holistic benefit-cost analysis of holding plebiscites on the EU accession of the various countries at a later date look like?

Proposals

1. Inclusion in the UN Charter: the group/collective human right of every population of a country to be able to vote on the constitution of the state in a plebiscite.

2. Inclusion in the UN Charter: the group/collective human right to secede from a state or unite with another state

---

[11] By holistic (=totological) I understand a comparison of the welfare of these countries in political, social, economic, scientific and cultural respects.

49

a) when, for instance, 20% (the percentage is subject to agreement) of the population of a territory is in favour of a referendum on secession or union, this must be held under UN supervision;

b) when in the referendum, for instance, 75 % (a different percentage is also possible) of the population is in favour of the proposal, the latter is to be implemented within a reasonable period.

3. As a new provision in the EU agreements:

a) In all countries of the EU where this has not yet happened, plebiscites will be held retroactively about membership of the EU.

b) Countries whose populations have not voted to remain in the EU with the required majority leave the EU.

c) New countries will only be admitted to the EU when their populations have voted for it in a plebiscite with a qualified majority.

4. In Germany

a) The Grundgesetz [Basic Law] should be replaced by a constitution which has received a qualified majority vote of the population in a plebiscite.

b) In elaborating the constitution, the experience of other countries, particularly Switzerland, should be evaluated.

c) It is to be verified if referenda should play a greater role on all political levels in the new constitution, e.g in the election of the head of state.

e) If this has not already happened, the constitution of every German federal state should be revised with regard to plebiscitary elements and then voted on in a referendum.

Thesis 7. Fair rules for international competition of ideologies should be established worldwide and enforced by the UNO.

Proposals

1. Condemnation of offensive military force except with UN mandate.

2. Ban and prosecution of all organisations which propagate, support and practice force in national politics.

3. Sanctions against countries which do not cooperate in prosecuting such organisations.

4. Extension of the offence of violation of human rights to all acts of violence on ideological or ethical grounds.

5. End to discrimination on ideological grounds.

6. Step-by-step opening of countries to those ideologies which accept the above rules of competition and support their observation.

Thesis 8. Democracy and free-market economy are important transitional forms on the way to the millennium.

Open ´questions

1. How are we to judge the liberalizing of the Chinese economy with the maintenance of the Communist Party's monopoly of power from the point of view of economic welfare? Have broad swathes of the population benefited from it with regard to their quality of life?

2. What successes can the fight against corruption demonstrate in democracies in comparison with totalitarian systems, if it takes place in these at all?

(China, for instance, would be a totalitarian system in which fighting corruption is at least officially an issue.)

Thesis 9. Democrats of the world unite!

Open questions

1. What does the global up and down of human rights, multiculturalism, pluralism, free market economy and democracy look like since the French revolution up to the present?

2. What does it look like for the individual continents and countries?

3. How are antiquity, the middle Ages and the modern age up to 1789 to be judged in this regard?

4. How does the Attic democracy under Pericles rate in this respect?

5. How many countries and how many people in total are currently ruled by totalitarian regimes?

6. What are the minimum criteria to be met for a political system to be called democratic? How many countries with how many people in total meet these criteria?

7. How does the present network of international organisations within the UNO function and cooperate? I am thinking of NATO, G7, G20, OECD, World Bank, International Monetary Fund, etc. and the major unions of countries, such as the EU, ASEAN, etc.

Proposals

1. Establishment of a group of all democratic countries in the world, if possible, analogous to the G7 but with broader objectives. Fields of cooperation could be action in favour of human rights and democracy, possibly in collabouration with Amnesty International, further development of democratic structures,[12] coordination of development aid, support of

---

[12] Several proposals for this were presented elsewhere in this book. The acceptance of democracy leaves much to be desired in democratic countries as well, as is shown by a recent study by Infratest-Dimap commissioned by the Free University of Berlin: more than 60% of Germans are of the opinion that there is no real democracy in Germany. (Cf. the Freie Presse newspaper, 2.24.2015, p. 5.)

UNO peace-keeping forces, support of other UNO programs, relief of NATO and the USA, improvement of global environmental policy, etc.

2. Further democratic development of the group outlined in point 1 to a Union of Democratic States (UDS).

Thesis 10. Economic progress should not have losers in the long run.

Open Question

In terms of economic history, can a connection be scientifically proved between the pace, steadiness, balance and sustainability of developments, on the one hand, and restrictions related to labour law and the environment, on the other?

Thesis 11. The Marxist principle 'From each according to his ability, to each according his need' can only be realized in a civilization charachterised by love.

Open questions

1. In a civilisation in which all members have a fundamental attitude of love, must it <u>necessarily</u> come to the realisation of the principle 'From each according to his ability, to each according to his need'?

2. Is this <u>independent</u> of the legal, economic or social system ruling in the civilisation concerned as long as loving acts are not expressly forbidden?

3 .To what extent can the United Order be realised without God's help, for instance in an atheist society?

4. What conditions have to be met for the United Order to be realised in a family or business enterprise?

I. General Remarks

Why this short version of "Centuries After Luther"?

Not everybody has the time to read a philosophical book of 300 pages. Yet she or he should have the possibility to get an impression of the theses of the author with the arising questions and the derived proposals, so that she or he can enter into a discussion about them.

Luther in his time, the world five centuries later and the future perspective.

The 500th anniversary of the Reformation in 2017 was celebrated globally as a significant event for many good reasons. Even the Catholic Church could have celebrated it as well, because the reformation process has eliminated some grave deficits within that church since Luther's time. The question as to whether it would have done this at all or within the same time frame is hard to answer. At any rate, Luther may be honoured as a potential martyr: he was ready to die for his convictions. His death as a martyr was only prevented by the power constellation of that time and the protection of the Electors of Saxony. The utterance ascribed to him – which he may, however, not actually have made – has marked the destiny of trend-setting personalities from all ideologies throughout the centuries up until the present: 'Here I stand. I can do no other. God help me. Amen.' This statement might also have been the motto of Jesus Christ Himself, whose servant Martin Luther rightly considered himself to be. If we leave out the second part 'God help me. Amen' this utterance also marks the behaviour of millions of believers of other faiths and atheists who have risked their lives for their convictions over the centuries of human history, and are still doing so in our time. I am thinking of dissidents of all shades in the totalitarian systems from Adam on.

The fact that the publication of Luther's 95 theses had its 500th anniversary in 2017 did in fact inspire me to write this book. Nevertheless, there are several reasons why my theses are only to be understood as a comment on Luther's theses to a very minor extent. Luther's theses are mainly concerned directly or indirectly with the practice of that time of buying remission of sins with letters of indulgence. This deficiency no longer plays a role in the Catholic Church of today and therefore needs no further comment. In my writings I agree with Luther's fundamental statements on the subject of sin and grace with some restrictions and attempt to place them in a broader context. Furthermore, a considerable number of Luther's theses deal with the role of the papacy at that time. On this point, there have likewise certainly been changes, the extent of which I am not able to assess fully and do not wish to comment on as a non-Catholic, since this is an internal problem of the Catholic Church.

Luther's theses are completely within the context of his time, which was marked by the largely uncontested rule of the clergy and the Catholic Church's strong political influence in the Europe of that time. The important parallels to my theses are to be found here. I likewise see the latter in a close context of the time in which they were written, which is, however, after five centuries, marked by secularism and a global ideological pluralism. Seen globally, there is thus not a single ruling ideology in the background but a large variety of ideologies from atheism to world religions and numerous other minor currents. I confront this secular, pluralistic world with the claim from ancient and latter-day Christian revelation that Jesus Christ is the God of the whole Earth and that all philosophy and science, art and politics converge in Him and His doctrine. Instead of ideological conflict, I advocate an "ideological cooperation" and a restoration of all that is good and true from all epochs of human history.

I am not alone in my perspective. It has been the historical viewpoint of Latter-day Saints since Joseph Smith (1806-

1844): we find ourselves in the epoch of the fullness of times. It is the last great epoch of human history prior to the second coming of Jesus Christ. This is what I have in mind when I draw conclusions for philosophical and scientific issues of our time on a theological basis. These are entirely my own personal views and not the standpoint of any church or organisation.

It is clear to me that many people will say that I am turning back the wheel of history. I would answer with a modification of this image: history resembles a running race that started in a stadium and will end in a stadium, like the marathon at the Olympic Games. I already thematised this perspective with regard to Jesus Christ's thousand-year reign in the following poem, which was published in German in 1976:

The stadium is already beckoning

Twittering of birds and beating of wings.
Even the roaring of squadrons is drowned.
Children are playing in the garden in front of the house.
At the window a tulip is flirting with a crocus.
Is morning still going round in a circle?

Contours are bathing in milky mist,
melting into the eye over floods of tears.
Buds have already swollen up
to fling out the blossom
before the face of the world.
Is the circle already casting spirals?

By the surging sea the city is greening,
and where the wilderness still dwells,
a garden is ready to bloom.
Soft currents are streaming into the lake.
Women are camping on the shore,
where a lion is crying its first tears
because the sweet lamb is sprawling before it.

The stadium is already beckoning,
in which the circle is rotating,
in which the race will end.

(From Bruno Johannsson (2017): Come. Poems. Eliza Editions 1. Translation from the German by Hilary Teske, Twenty Six in the Publishing Group Random House, Norderstedt, p. 58)

The inner logic of "Centuries After Luther"

My reflections are based on theological convictions (cf. Theses 1 to 30), which are, however, only partially questioned, proved or substantiated. This "partially" already results alone from the essay style, which dominates the main text. Neither should the extensive footnotes lead to the false conclusion that the theses are scientific, theological deductions in a strict sense. This is not the case, simply because I did not systematically take account of all the theological discussions within Christianity during the past centuries.

The theological basis which is my starting point is itself, in turn, founded on the canon of Judeo-Christian scriptural records. In single cases, I am able to take a brief look at Islamic and Hindu thinking. However, this is extremely limited due to my lack of intensive study of the scriptures of these religions up to now. By Christian canon I understand first of all the Old and New Testaments as sources of "ancient revelation". In addition, there are the standard Latter-day Saint works, which I classify as holy scripture and occasionally call "new revelation". They consist of the Book of Mormon, the Book of Doctrine and Covenants and the Pearl of Great Price (see Bibliography).

Concerning the books of the Bible, I am aware that the problems of scriptural records and translation are mostly rather difficult. The numerous translators have sometimes taken great liberties so that I have decided to use the interlinear translations from Hebrew and Greek available in the German language. From this they were translated as literally as possible into English. The result sometimes differs from the King James Bible.

As far as the reliability of the mentioned sources is concerned, evaluating them is ultimately an act of faith from case to case, requiring inspiration. I cite the witnesses of Christian theology over the centuries to testify to the fact that the books of the Bible are, for the most part, sources to be taken seriously. As an outstanding individual personality in this host of witnesses, I would first of all like to mention Martin Luther, who translated the Bible into German. I also appreciate the work of the 47 scholars who worked on the King James Version of the Bible. Another important witness for me is Joseph Smith, who corrected and supplemented parts of the King James Version but fundamentally accepted it. Last but not least, my respect goes to by the Catholic-Protestant commission that in 1980 produced the Einheitsübersetzung [standardised German Bible translation], which is also approved and used by Latter-day Saints in Germany. For the Old Testament there is the additional testimony of Jewish theologians of past centuries. Also Jesus Christ Himself and John, Peter and Paul directly or indirectly recognised and referred to the Books of Moses and the prophets Isaiah, Jeremiah, etc. However, I not only want to list the Messiah, His prophets, priests and scribes as witnesses but also millions of "simple" believers, who over the centuries have borne testimony in word and deed to the validity of the holy scriptures. Seen from this perspective, I am not alone when I basically trust these sources and derive my theological foundation for reflections on philosophy and various sciences from them. Nevertheless, there is no doubt that the foundation of this book is faith and not science in the meaning of this concept in our time.

When I present Christian theology filtered by transmission and translation as the quasi axiomatic basis of my reflections, I am aware that it is an unusually complex and problematic basis in a logical sense. However, I can mitigate this situation by reducing the whole of Christian doctrine to one person and one principle – the person of Jesus Christ and the principle of love. As I will explain in more detail, they are like two sides of one and the same coin. In the principle of love, the whole of Christian doctrine relating to the diversity of life is reduced to a single principle, as Jesus Himself formulated it in Matthew 22:40. In the person of Christ, in turn, this principle is perfectly embodied and realised, as John says in his first epistle 1 John 4:16: "God is love..." Through this reduction, which is firmly prescribed in Christian tradition, the axiomatic basis of my reflections again becomes very straightforward.

In deducing consequences for individual scientific disciplines, we arrived at the selective contributions in this book on the theory of knowledge, theory of science, cosmology, anthropology, psychology, medicine, aesthetics, sociology, economics and political science. In three cases we might speak of relatively new paradigms, which are fit to be theoretical foundations for further scientific research. This first of all concerns a theory of spirit lying between natural science and esotericism (cf. Chapter D). Furthermore, a comprehensive concept of a theory of civilisation is proposed (cf. Chapter I). My ethical reflections also have a fundamental character without claiming to be novel individually (cf. Chapter H).

As the essay form has been selected, the reader naturally cannot expect a logically exact deduction, as was tendentially the case, for instance, in medieval scholasticism or – on a different basis – with Ludwig Wittgenstein. Whilst every word is, in principle, significant for me in the formulation of the individual theses, the subsequent essay is marked by a relatively spontaneous orbiting round the theses. I may sometimes also lose sight of my theological basis to some extent. However, I hope that it repeatedly becomes noticeable as food for thought and as a corrective vis-à-vis the prevailing theories in the fields of the philosophical disciplines and individual sciences listed above.

At this point, I would like to address a word to those of my readers who have neither emotional nor intellectual access to the Christian way of thinking, particularly that of Latter-day Saints. I have complete understanding if they lay down my book immediately. On the other hand, it would be absolutely conceivable that they might benefit from reading it and possibly even realise that in deducing my consequences for the individual sciences I sometimes reach similar conclusions as, for example, a Catholic theologian, an orthodox Jew, a Muslim or an atheistic humanist. The spectrum I cover in this book in fact ranges from Jesus Christ over Martin Luther and Joseph Smith to Karl Marx.

Invitation to disputation

"Out of love for the truth and from desire to elucidate it, the Reverend Father Martin Luther, Master of Arts and Sacred Theology, and ordinary lecturer therein at Wittenberg, intends to defend the following statements and to dispute on them in that place. Therefore he asks that those who cannot be present and dispute with him orally shall do so in their absence by letter. In the name of our Lord Jesus Christ, Amen."[13] These are the words with which Luther introduced his theses, as was consistent with the academic custom of his epoch. Times and customs have changed and nowadays live disputations rarely take place at universities, apart from the doctoral examination procedure. Technical communication possibilities now move in completely new paths due to the development of the Iinternet and they have also been used in this project to a certain extent. The existing version of this book is intended to undergo a significant improvement with the aid of its readers. First of all, every reader is invited to send comments, criticism, proposals for improvement, bibliographical references including scriptural references, etc. to Bruno.Johannsson@freenet.de. Please do not forget to state the chapter (A to K), thesis number and, if possible, the number of the paragraph within the essay (not indicated in the text). The latter is, of course, only necessary when the comment relates to a concrete passage of text.

If the feedback exceeds a certain amount, the author reserves the possibility not to react to all the argumentation in detail. At his advanced age, this is a matter of time and ener-

---

[13] http://www.luther.de/en/95thesen.html (2015)

gy. However, at this point I would like to express my warmest thanks to those who have taken time to read my book and give feedback. Should a reader succeed in prompting the author to change a thesis or an essay on a thesis, they will in any case be informed and mentioned by name in the second edition of the book unless they expressly ask for this not to be done. The second – and hopefully considerably improved version of this book – is to be published on October 31, 2017 if possible. It is hoped that it will be a document for the ideological cooperation I advocate in the book.

The above invitation to a process of communication will hopefully also make it clear to the reader that I am aware of the following fact: I do not know what I do not know and today consider some things to be knowledge which will one day prove to be errors. The limits of my knowledge are also indicated by the questions found at the end of most of the essays. They are an invitation to the reader to let me have this information. If this knowledge does not exist at all, it is an invitation to researchers to instigate appropriate projects.

A significant deepening of the critical reflection in some of my individual theses already exists in the form of 32 long philosophical live dialogues conducted and recorded by Thea Johansson and myself in the last few years. They are now published in five volumes which are available worldwide through www.amazon.com. If you enter "Thea and Bruno Johannsson" all five volumes are presented with reading samples and the details of the print and e-book editions. In the philosophical dialogues, Thea and I have taken turns in playing the role of midwife in the Socratic sense and helped bring a large number of our thoughts to light.

The possibility of disputation is given on my English Site https://.bruno-johannsson.jimdofree.com/contact. As far as my time permits I will be eager to answer and to discuss. Thea Johannsson will help me though she has another opinion in quite a number of subjects.

Thea Johannsson also read the present work and influenced it by making numerous comments. Besides her, there was only one other person who had a view of the entire text and pointed out some errors: this was Hilary Teske, who was ready to translate the book into English without having any guarantee that an interested publisher would be found. Thanks to her, it is hoped that this work will be published in German and English almost simultaneously.

My special thanks go to Prof. Dr. Herbert Giersch and Prof. Dr. Olaf Sievert, two of my academic role models who have practised and familiarised me with the not so widespread thinking in theses; they both worked at the Saarland University and were both long-standing Chairmen of the Board of Experts for the Assessment of Macroeconomic Development.

Last but not least my thanks go to my Father in Heaven, to his Son Jesus Christ and to the Holy Ghost who have exercised their special kind of cooperation to influence me in writing this book. In many, many prayers I have tried to secure this influence. Yet the probability is high that there are still mistakes in it. Please put them down to my personal weakness and let me know your opinion on the website above.

Bruno Johannsson   September 2021

IV. Bibliography

Holy Scripture

Old Testament
  Steurer, Rita Maria (1967 to 2012): Das Alte Testament [The Old Testament]. Hebrew-German interlinear translation and transcription of the original text according to the Biblia Hebraica Stuttgartiensis, five volumes published in different years (see above) and editions, Hänssler-Verlag, Neuhausen-Stuttgart, (These five volumes were not published in the order of the biblical canon. In the volume "Joshua to Kings" the editor omitted to assign the volume a number. Logically, it should be volume 2.) In the notes I refer with the abbreviation "Old Testament" to the volume in which the corresponding Hebrew-German book is printed. The English text is a literal translation of the German text.

New Testament
  Dietzfelbinger, Ernst, Das Neue Testament [The New Testament], Greek-German interlinear translation according to the Nestle-Aland version, 26th edition, translated by Ernst Dietzfelbinger,1986, Hänssler-Verlag, Neuhausen-Stuttgart. In the notes I use the abbreviation "New Testament". The English text is a literal translation of the German text.

  Other translations of the Bible occasionally mentioned:
  Directmedia (publisher),2004, Biblia, Das ist: Die gantze Heilige Schrift: Deutsch. Auffs new zugericht von D. Martin Luther,1545, Digitale Bibliothek, Vol 29, Directmedia, Berlin
  The Holy Bible, Containing the Old and New Testaments, translated out of the original tongues: And with the former translations diligently compared and revised, by his Majesty's special command. (King James Version).

65

Die Bibel, Altes und Neues Testament, Einheitsüberset-zung, 1980, Katholische Bibelanstalt, , Herder, Freiburg-Basel-Wien

Die fünf Bücher der Weisung, [The Five Books of Instruc-tion], German translation by Martin Buber together with Franz Rosenzweig, 10th revised edition of the amended edi-tion of 1954, 4 Volumes, Vol. 1, p. 206, 1992, published by the Deutsche Bibelgesellschaft, Stuttgart.)

Book of Mormon

The Church of Jesus Christ of Latter-day Saints (publish-er), The Book of Mormon, An Account Written by the Hand of Mormon upon Plates taken from the Plates of Nephi, Translated by Joseph Smith, Jun., 1830/1976, Salt Lake City, Utah, USA. In the notes this work is referred to in its abbrevi-ated form "Book of Mormon"

Doctrine and Covenants

The Church of Jesus Christ of Latter-day Saints (publish-er), The Doctrine and Covenants of the Church of Jesus Christ of Latter-day Saints, Containing Revelations Given to Joseph Smith, the Prophet With some Additions by his Successors in the Presidency of the Church. 1835/1976, Salt Lake City, Utah, USA. In the notes this work is referred to in its abbrevi-ated form as "Doctrine and Covenants"

Pearl of Great Price

The Church of Jesus Christ of Latter-day Saints (publish-er), *The Pearl of Great Price*. A Selection from the Revela-tions, Translations and Narrations of Joseph Smith, First Prophet, Seer and Revelator to the Church of Jesus Christ of Latter-day Saints, 1851/1976, Salt Lake City, Utah, USA. In the notes this work is referred to in its abbreviated form as "Pearl of Great Price".

Other sources

Abbot, Edwin A., Flächenland. Ein mehrdimensionaler Roman verfasst von einem alten Quadrat, 1884/1982, Klett-Cotta, Stuttgart

Alexander, Eben, Blick in die Ewigkeit, 3rd edition, 2012/2013, Ansata Verlag, Munich

Allred, Gordon (editor), God the Father,1979, Deseret Book Company, Salt Lake City

Arrington, Leonhard J. Great Basin Kingdom. An Economic History of the Latter-day Saints 1830-1900., 1958/1966, University of Nebraska Press, Lincoln-London

Arrington, Leonhard J./Fox, Feramorz Y./May, Dean L., Building the City of God. Community and Cooperation among the Mormons, 1976, Deseret Book Company, Salt Lake City

Augustine, Confessions, approx 400 AD, translated by Edward Bouverie Pusey, sacred-texts.com.

Barker, James L., Apostasy from the Divine Church, 1960/1984, Bookcraft, Salt Lake City

Benson, Ezra Taft, The Great Commandment – Love the Lord, Ensign, May 1988

Benson, Ezra Taft, Jesus Christ – Our Savior and Redeemer, Ensign, June 1990

Brinzanik, Roman/Hülswith, Tobias (editors), Werden wir ewig leben? – Gespräche über die Zukunft von Mensch und Technologie, 2010, Suhrkamp, Berlin

Buber, Martin, Erzählungen von Engeln, Geistern und Dämonen, 2nd edition, 1994, Verlag Lambert Schneider, Gerlingen

Bushman, Richard Lyman, Joseph Smith – Rough Rolling Stone, 2005, Alfred A. Knopf, New York

Coase, R. H, The Problem of Social Cost, Journal of Law and Economics, Vol. 3, 1960, pp. 1-44

Clouse, Robert (editor), Das Tausendjährige Reich: Bedeutung und Wirklichkeit. Vier Beiträge aus evangelikaler

Sicht, 1977/1983, Verlag der Francke-Buchhandlung, Marburg

Davidson, John, Natural Creation and the Formative Mind, 1991, Element Books Ltd., Shaftesbury, Dorset, England

Davidson, John, Am Anfang ist der Geist. Die Geburt von Materie und Leben aus dem schöpferischen Geist, 1994, Otto Wilhelm Barth Verlag, Bern-Munich-Vienna

Dawkins, Richard, The God Delusion, 2006, Bantam Books

Elias, Norbert, Über den Prozess der Zivilisation. Sozialgenetische und psychogenetische Untersuchungen, 2 volumes, 1939/2010, Suhrkamp, Berlin

Emmott, Stephen, Ten Billion, 2013, Vintage Books/Random House

Fine, Cordelia: Wissen Sie, was ihr Gehirn denkt? Wie in unserem Oberstübchen die Wirklichkeit verzerrt wird...und warum, 2007. Springer Spektrum, Heidelberg

Gitt, Werner, Logos oder Chaos. Aussagen und Einwände zur Evolutionslehre sowie eine tragfähige Alternative, 1980, Hänssler-Verlag, Neuhausen-Stuttgart

Goschke, Thomas, Wie wir entscheiden. Erkenntnisse aus Psychologie und Neurowissenschaft, lecture in the German Hygiene Museum in Dresden on 26.2.2013

Goethe, Johann Wolfgang von, Faust, a tragedy, 1831, German and English side-by-side translations: Priest, Brooks and Coleridge, 2013

Huntington, Samuel P, The Clash of Civilisations and the Remaking of World Order, 1996, Simon & Schuster, New York

Jank, Horst Henning, Georgien. Institutioneller Wandel und wirtschaftliche Entwicklung, 2000, Technical University of Cottbus, Cottbus

Johannsson, Bruno, Ich liebe dich, wenn ich mich liebe. Ich liebe mich, wenn ich dich liebe. Zum Verhältnis von Eigen- und Nächstenliebe, Essay, 2014, http://philosophy-slam.de/ich-liebe-dich-wenn-ich-mich-liebe,

Johannsson, Bruno and Thea, Spielregeln der Gesellschaft. Philosophical dialogues. Unpublished manuscript

Johannsson, Thea, Screwtape schreibt wieder, unpublished manuscript, 2012

Kaiser, Stephan/Ringlstetter, Max et al., Creating Balance? International Perspectives on the Work-Life Integration of Professionals, 2011, Springer, Berlin. For discussion cf. also http://de.wikipedia.org/Work-Life-Balance.

Kant, Immanuel, Critique of Practical Reason, 1799, Project Gutenberg, translation by Thomas Kingsmill Abbott, 2003

Kleist, Heinrich von,1810/1985,, Michael Kohlhaas. short story, Kleist's works in two volumes, vol 1, Aufbau Verlag, Berlin-Weimar, p. 80 ff.

Koch, Christof, Das Nicht-Bewusste oder der Zombie in uns, in Andreas Sentker / Frank Wigger (editors), Rätsel Ich. Gehirn, Gefühl, Bewusstsein, 2007, Springer-Verlag and Zeit-Verlag, Berlin-Heidelberg, pp. 267 – 279

Knoblauch, Hubert, Berichte aus dem Jenseits. Mythos und Realität der Nahtoderfahrung, 1999, Herder-Verlag, Freiburg

Knoblauch, Hubert / Soeffner, Hans-Georg (editors): Todesnähe. Interdisziplinäre Beiträge zu einem außergewöhnlichen Phänomen, 1999, Universitätsverlag Konstanz, Constance

Kübler-Ross, Elisabeth, Interviews mit Sterbenden, 1969, Kreuz-Verlag, Stuttgart

Larson, Andrew Karl, "I Was Called to Dixie": The Virgin River Basin: Unique Experiences on Mormon Pioneering, 1961/1992, Dixie College Foundation, St. George, Utah

Leibniz, G. W., The Monadology, translation by George MacDonald Ross, 1999

Lewis, C. S., The Screwtape Letters, 1942, Geoffrey Bles

Lommel, Pim van, Endloses Bewusstsein. Neue medizinische Fakten zur Nahtoderfahrung, 2007/2009, Patmos, Düsseldorf

Lund, Gerald N., The Coming of the Lord, 1971/1980, 15th edition, Bookcraft, Salt Lake City

Luther, Martin: 95 Theses in Luther's Works, 55 volumes 1517/1957.1986, various translators, St. Louis, Minneapolis, Concordia Publishing House, Fortress Press

Luther, Martin, Interpretation of the seven psalms on repentance, tract, in A manual of the Book of psalms, Or, The Subject-contents of All the Psalms, translation by Henry Cole, London, R.B. Seeley and W. Burnside, 1517/1837

Luther, Martin, On Christian Freedom, tract, 1520, translation by H. Wace and C.A. Buckheim, in First Principles of the Reformation, Philadelphia, 1520/1885, translation based on the Erlangen Edition (1828-70) of Luther's Collected Works

Marx, Karl, Capital, A Critique of Political Economy, Volume I, Book One: The Process of Production of Capital, Part 1, Chapter 1, Section 5. 1867/1887, translation by Samuel Moore and Edward Aveling, edited by Frederick Engels

Marx, Karl, marginalia in the program of the German Workers' Party, Section 1, 1975/2014. This brief text was embedded in a letter, was published posthumously by Engels and is called "Kritik des Gothaer Programms (Critique of the Gotha Program]". (Cf.: wikipedia.org/wiki/Critique.of the Gotha Program, accessed on 17.7.2014)

Mathur, Vijay K, "How Well Do We Know Pareto Optimality?", 1991, Journal of Economic Education,Vol. 22,No. 2

McConkie, Bruce R., Mormon Doctrine, second edition, 1979, Bookcraft, Salt Lake City

McConkie, Bruce R., The Millennial Messiah. The Second Coming of the Son of Man, 1982, Deseret Book Company, Salt Lake City

McGrath, Allister, The Dawkins Delusion. Atheist Fundamentalism and the denial of the divine, 2007, Society for the Promotion of Christian Knowledge, UK

Moody, Raymond A, Reflections on Life after Life, 1977, Bantam Books, New York

Mouritsen, Dale C., The Spiritual World – Our Next Home, Ensign, January 1977, pp. 47 – 51

Nagel, Thomas, Geist und Kosmos. Warum die materialistische neodarwinistische Konzeption der Natur so gut wie sicher falsch ist, 2013, Suhrkamp, Berlin

Peterson, Martin, An Introduction to Decision Theory, 2009, Cambridge University Press, Cambridge

Plato, Theory of Eros in the Symposion, approx.. 380 BC/1979, published by Wiley, Vol. 13, No 1, pp 67-75

Piketty, Thomas, Capital in the Twenty-First Century. 2013/2014, Harvard University Press, Cambridge

Popper, Karl. R./Eccles, John C., The Self and Its Brain, 1977, Springer International, New York

Precht, Richard David. Wer bin ich – und wenn ja wie viele? Eine philosophische Reise, 2007, Wilhelm Goldmann Verlag, Munich

Sarrazin, Thilo. Deutschland schafft sich ab. Wie wir unser Land aufs Spiel setzen, 2010, Deutsche Verlagsanstalt, Munich

Schiller, Friedrich, On Grace and Dignity, translation by George Gregory, 1793/1992, Schiller Institute, p. 368

Schmid, Wilhelm, Die Geburt der Philosophie im Garten der Lüste. Michel Foucaults Archäologie des platonischen Eros, 2000,Suhrkamp, Frankfurt a. M.

Sedlácek, Tomás, 2009, Economics of Good and Evil. The Quest for Economic Meaning from Gilgamesh to Wall Street, 2009/2011, Oxford University Press, Oxford

Sen, Amartya. Collective Choice and Social Welfare, 1970.Holden-Day, San-Francisco

Sen, Amartya, The Standard of Living. Tanner Lectures in Human Values, 1987, The Press Syndicate of the University of Cambridge, Cambridge.

Sen, Amartya, On Economic Inequality. 1997, Clarendon Press, Oxford

Sen, Amartya, Rationality and freedom. 2002, Belknap Press, Cambridge, Massachusetts

Sen, Amartya, Identity and Violence: The Illusion of Destiny, 2007, W. Norton & Company

Sen, Amartya/ Stiglitz, Joseph E/ Fitoussi, Jean-Pau, The Measurement of Economic Performance and Social Progress Revisited: Reflections and Overview. Document de travail OFCE, [French Economic Observatory working paper], 2009

Sen, Amartya, Peace and democratic society, 2011,Open Book Publishers, Cambridge, England

Sentker, Andreas/Wigger, Frank (editors), Rätsel Ich. Gehirn, Gefühl, Bewusstsein, 2007, Springer-Verlag and Zeit-Verlag, Berlin-Heidelberg

Sentker, Andreas/Wigger, Frank (editors). Schaltstelle Gehirn. Denken Erkennen, Handeln., 2008, Springer-Verlag and Zeit-Verlag, Berlin-Heidelberg

Sievert, Olaf/ Naust, Hermann/Jochum, Dieter/ Peglow, Michael/Glumann, Thorolf, Steuern und Investitionen, Vol. 1, 1989, Verlag Peter Lang, Frankfurt a. M.

Smith, Joseph, Gods Many and Lords Many, 1844, in Allred, Gordon (editor), God the Father, 1979, Deseret Book Company, Salt Lake City, pp. 244-253

Smith, Joseph, The King Follet Discourse,1844, in Allred, Gordon (editor), God the Father, 1979, Deseret Book Company, Salt Lake City, pp. 222-243

Stiglitz, Joseph, Globalization and Its Discontents, 2002, W. W. Norton & Company, USA

Swami, A. C. Bhaktivedanta.Teachings of Lord Chaitanya. A Treatise on Factual Spiritual Life, 1968, International Society for Krishna Consciousness, New York

The Church of Jesus Christ of Latter-day Saints (editor), Hymns, 1985, Salt Lake City, Utah, USA

The Church of Jesus Christ of Latter-day Saints (editor/publisher), Teachings of the Presidents of the Church: Brigham Young, 1997, Salt Lake City, Utah, USA

The Church of Jesus Christ of Latter-day Saints (/publisher), Teachings of the Presidents of the Church: Joseph Smith, 2007, Salt Lake City, Utah, USA

The Church of Jesus Christ of Latter-day Saints (publisher), Teachings of the Presidents of the Church: Lorenzo Snow, 2912, Salt Lake City, Utah, USA

The Church of Jesus Christ of Latter-day Saints, Becoming like God, 2014, www.lds.org/topics/becoming-like-god

The Deseret Book Company (publisher), History of the Church of Jesus Christ of Latter-day Saints, seven volumes, introduction and notes by B. H. Roberts, second edition revised, 1976, Deseret Book, Salt Lake City

The Quran, in quran.com

Tolstoy, Leo, The Resurrection, novel, 1900, Oxford's World Classics

Uchtdorf, Dieter. F., You can do it now. Ensign, November 2013, p. 55

Wagoner, Richard S. Van. Mormon Polygamy. A History. 1986, Signature Books, Salt Lake City

Wedekind, Beate, Nagaya heißt Frieden. Karlheinz Böhm und seine Äthiopienhilfe Menschen für Menschen, 2006, Rütten & Loening, Berlin

Weizsäcker, Carl Friedrich von/Gopi Krishna von Crotona, Biologische Basis religiöser Erfahrung, 1971, Otto-Wilhelm-Barth-Verlag, Weilheim

Wikipedia – the free encyclopedia:
http://de.wikipedia.org/Work-Life-Balance
http://de.wikipedia.org/wiki/Kritik_des_Gothaer_Progr

Wittgenstein, Ludwig, Tractatus logico-philosophicus. Logisch–philosophische Abhandlung, 1921/1963, edition suhrkamp 12, Suhrkamp, Frankfurt a. M.

V. Appendix

The original work, from which the upper theses, questions and proposals have been extracted:

Bruno Johannsson

Centuries After Luther

A Christian Manifest in a Pluralistic and Globalized World

Translated from the German by Hilary Teske

eBook and paperback, 300 pp. ISBN: 9 983740 772765

More details and reading samples on your country website of Amazon or other online bookstores.

Unlike Luther, who published his theses in a Catholic Europe in 1517, the author refers in 95 theses to the globalized and pluralistic world of our times. Each thesis is explained with a generally understandable essay of 2-5 pages. Numerous remarks allow readers with scientific interests to go into greater depth. At the end of most theses questions are formulated showing that the author knows what he does not know. At the end of some theses proposals for political action are made such as fighting hunger, diminishing inequality, promoting democracy and reforming the United Nations.

Johannsson starts by outlining his conservative sight of Christian theology based on the Bible and some clarifying revelations of Joseph Smith (1806 – 1844). In the following ten chapters the author attempts to show the great relevance of Christian theology for the questions of our time. He indicates the possibility of a compromise between creationism and evolution theory. His theory of matter, spirit and soul has the potential of bringing natural and social sciences nearer to each other. His concept of Christian love proves not only to be a fundamental principle of ethics but also of economics and political science.

The poetical approach to the Second Coming of Jesus Christ
Bruno Johannsson

Come

Poems, Eliza Editions 1
Translated from the German by Hilary Teske
94 pp, hardbound, softbound and eBook editions available
ISBN: 978-3-740730-659, 973-3-740744-496, ASIN:B07856L43K
Details and reading samples in most online bookstores and on
https://bruno-johannsson.jimdofree.com.

Here some excerpts from reviews:

A volume of poetry that reveals the beauty of its structure only in a repeated reading but then it should be possible for the attentive reader to find in all these poems his fears as well as his hopes, but also his tasks. (Prof. Dr. Sigrid Lichtenberger, University of Saarland, Department of German Studies.)

'Come' has accompanied me for weeks - always also in the cross-reading of the German version - and has appealed very strongly. Hilary Reske is a brilliant translator. Her extraordinary linguistic and poetic talent lets the poems often appear less like a translation, but more as a work that could stand on its own. The presentation of the volume is beautifully done: whether it's the format or the way the book feels - both on the outside and when leafing through it or the attractive graphic design. The poems will certainly appeal to Christian readers first... Language and images make an exciting and challenging reading and inspire reflection. I would imagine that 'Come' will also appeal to German readers, who enjoy English literature...(Jürgen Fischer, Interpreter, Karlsruhe, Germany 2020)

Mr. Johannsson knows what it is to flounder. And when we read his poems, we can be glad of this, because he speaks for all of us who flounder, taking us to his quiet places, "a little lower than the angels", where confusions are valued and the answers we keep demanding matter less than celebrating the sacred riddles themselves. These verses speak to a Christian heart, and to any heart that longs for a better world and dares to have faith in a spiritual future...(Darl Mangelson, Chicago Illinois 2020)